Butterfly Eyes

To Jim, my life's companion, who walks with me through sun and rain
—J.S.

For my nieces and nephews
—B.K.

www.houghtonmifflinbooks.com

The text of this book is set in 14-point Legacy.
The illustrations are scratchboard.

Library of Congress Cataloging-in-Publication Data
Sidman, Joyce.
Butterfly eyes and other secrets of the meadow : poems / by Joyce Sidman ; illustrations by Beth Krommes.
p. cm.
ISBN 0-618-56313-X (hardcover)
1. Children's poetry, American. 2. Meadow animals—Juvenile poetry.
3. Meadows—Juvenile poetry. I. Krommes, Beth, ill. II. Title.
PS3569.I295M43 2006   811'.54—dc22   2005003921

ISBN-13: 978-0-618-56313-5

Manufactured in China
LEO 10 9 8 7 6 5 4 3 2 1

Butterfly Eyes

and Other Secrets
of the Meadow

written by JOYCE SIDMAN   illustrated by BETH KROMMES

HOUGHTON MIFFLIN COMPANY

BOSTON 2006

In the Almost-Light

In the dark,
in the night,
in the almost-light,
in the leaf-crisp air just before sunlight,
sprouts a secret, silent, sparkling sight:
berries grown on the vines of night.

On the grass,
on the buds,
on the bark of trees,
on the small clear wings of the bumblebees,
on the spiderwebs (and the spiders' knees),
come the jewels of the dawn
    in the cool night's breeze.

And the sun
when it comes
through the purple haze
touches each clear gem with its sidelong gaze,
fingers each clear drop with its lazy rays,
gathers each one back for the summer's days.

What is it?

Morning Warming

sun

sunwarm

sunwarm on back

sunwarm on back legs

sunwarm on back legs loosens

    my heart

    my heart beats

    my heart beats faster

in sunwarm my heart beats faster

      I flex

      I flex legs

      I flex legs loose with sunwarm

      I drink dew from dripping leaves

      I beat

         flex

            crouch

      leap!

What am I?

DEW AND GRASSHOPPER

On calm, clear summer nights, the meadow cools down quickly. Grasses, flowers, leaves, and even insects become cooler than the warm air around them. Just as it does on a cold can of soda pop, water vapor in the air condenses on those cool surfaces, forming dew. Then, as dawn comes and the sun touches them, the dew drops evaporate back into the air.

Grasshoppers also cool down and lose most of their body heat at night. They need the sun's warmth (and a drink of dew) to start moving again in the morning. Covered with a tough outer coating called an exoskeleton, their small bullet shape is streamlined for long-distance leaping. They use powerful back legs to jump up to twenty times their own length!

Shhh! They Are Sleeping

Shhh! They are small.
Shhh! They are many.
Shhh! In a heap, they lie soundly asleep.

Soft is their fur.
Soft are their noses.
Soft is the curl of their grassy nest-keep.

Eyes not quite open.
Ears in a tangle.
Paws folded close beneath whisker and chin.

Shhh! They are hidden.
Shhh! They are waiting.
Gathering strength for their life to begin.

What are they?

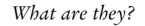

He

trots
through
meadow-gold grass
in dawn sun
     furred
     mysterious
a word
     hunting
     its own
meaning

Who is he?

RABBIT AND FOX

Dawn and dusk—the magical times between night and day—are also dangerous times for many creatures of the meadow. Some predators, such as the fox, use this time to hunt. With its incredible hearing, the fox will listen for the rustling of rabbits or mice. It will wait silently for its prey to appear; then, like a cat, it will jump high in the air and pounce.

To keep her young hidden from predators like the fox, the mother rabbit visits her babies only occasionally. Hairless and blind, baby rabbits (called kittens) huddle together in their snugly covered nests of grass and fur at the meadow's edge. The kits grow fast, and in only three weeks—now bright-eyed and furry— they are ready to sample the meadow's delights and dangers.

Bubble Song

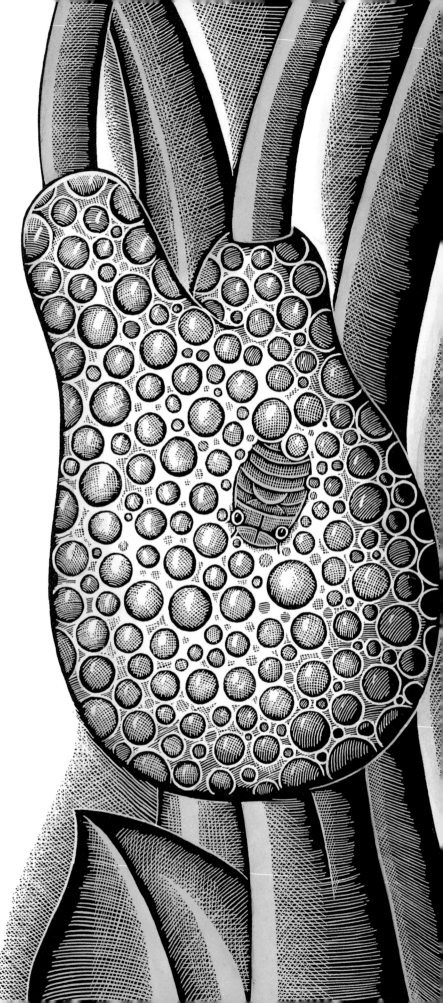

Beautiful bubbles
bubbles of pearl,
all in a clustery, bubbly swirl
Bubbles I blow
from my own bubble-spout
(I'll never
      I'll never
           I'll never come out!)

Beautiful bubbles
bubbles of foam
Bubbly castle,
snug bubble-home
keeps my skin tender
saves me from drought
(I'll never
      I'll never
           I'll never come out!)

Beautiful bubbles
bubbles of spume
guard me and hide me
in my bubble-room
Until I'm a grownup
and wings fully sprout
I'll never
      I'll never
           I'll never come out!

What am I?

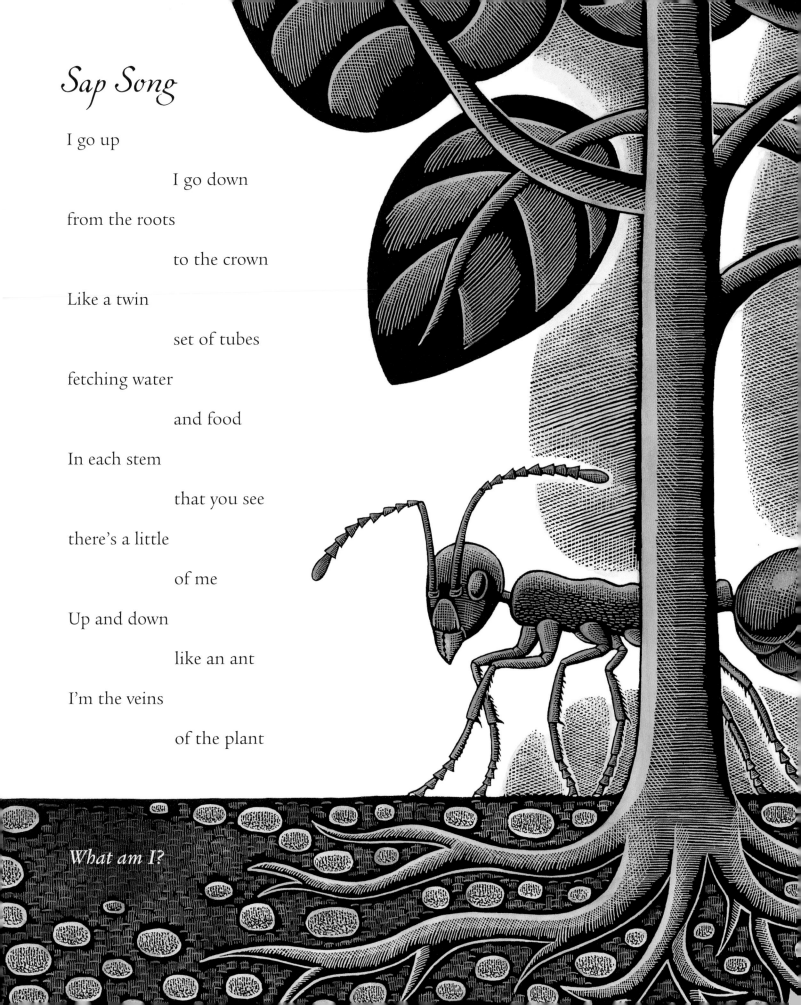

Sap Song

I go up

        I go down

from the roots

        to the crown

Like a twin

        set of tubes

fetching water

        and food

In each stem

        that you see

there's a little

        of me

Up and down

        like an ant

I'm the veins

        of the plant

What am I?

SPITTLEBUG AND XYLEM & PHLOEM

Have you ever seen a small glob of foam on a meadow plant? Inside that glob you'll find a ⅛-inch-long spittlebug, the nymph (young) form of an insect also called a froghopper. When spittlebugs hatch from eggs, they latch on to stems and suck sap from the plant. In the spittlebug's body, this sap is mixed with chemicals, then excreted and blown into a froth with a special nozzle on the tip of their abdomens. Until midsummer, when the spittlebug matures into an adult froghopper, it snuggles in its bubbly home, protected from predators, parasites, heat, and the strong summer sun.

Spittlebugs suck primarily xylem sap—the sap that comes up from a plant's roots. The xylem and phloem vessels are like the "veins" of a plant, carrying nutrients back and forth and helping to support the stem. Xylem tubes carry water and minerals upward. Phloem tubes carry the sugary food made by the leaves to all parts of the plant.

Heavenly

My pods are famous, of course:
soft green purses
on slim racks.

And my leaves: monarchs
adore them.
They plant their babies
and just fly away!

But have you ever
seen me *bloom*?
At high noon
on a midsummer's day
when the pavement is steeped in heat
and cicadas are screaming,
follow my heady perfume
and you will track me down:
see my
heavenly
        lavender
                muffins
baking in the sun.

What am I?

Ultraviolet

the eyes of these flies
see more than we see
they love scarlet
adore pink
thrive on orange
lap up yellow with
long curled tongues
but their favorite
extra-special secret
color sprinkled on
tiny wingscales
like valentines
and painted on the
most delectable blossoms
like bull's-eyes
that we can't see
because our eyes
are not theirs
is *ultraviolet*

What are they?

MILKWEED AND BUTTERFLIES

Milkweed is best known for its fluff-filled seedpods, but it is actually named for its milky sap, which is toxic to most insects and animals. Monarch butterflies are immune to these toxins and lay their eggs on the plant's leaves, which provide food for newly hatched caterpillars. By munching on milkweed, Monarch caterpillars (and later, butterflies) become bitter-tasting and even poisonous to most predators, which have learned to avoid them.

Butterflies serve a vital role as pollinators of meadow flowers. To attract them, flowers such as daisies and coneflowers are colored with eye-catching ultraviolet patterns that surround their pollen-filled centers. We can't see these patterns, but butterflies can: they have one of the widest ranges of color vision in the animal world. For them, ultraviolet colors—which also show up on their wings and help them identify each other—are like a secret language.

Letter to the Sun

Dear Sun:
It's so wet.

The meadow has turned to bog.
Chill, sinking, squishy sog.

We long for your face, Sun.
We crave your rays,
those
     long,
         lovely,
             honey-colored days.

O Dear Sun,
we're huddled in our buds,
waiting to bloom.

Please come soon . . .
the only ones still singing
are the frogs.

Signed, _____

Letter to the Rain

Dear Rain:
Sun has outstayed her welcome.

Grass is crunching,
berries shriveling,
the earth is a brick of dust.

Rain,
even the ants are tired.

We hate to bother you in this heat,
but could you send some of those
big
      fat
            drops
that splat and drum and puddle?

Even a drizzle would do.

Signed, _____

ONE AND ALL

Life in the meadow is always a balance. Drenching spring rains encourage seeds to sprout, insect eggs to hatch, and amphibians (such as frogs, toads, and salamanders) to mate. Summer sun warms the meadow and gives the plants energy to grow and flower. But too much sun can dry grasses and wildflowers, leaving them susceptible to disease. Frogs and worms, too, must have moisture to live, so they welcome the return of the rain. All meadow inhabitants need the sun, but they also need the rain.

Peel Deal

Glaze
days
itch
twitch
hot
spot
rub
slub
shed
head
rip
strip
squirm
worm
real
peel
skin
twin
sheen
Q
u
e
e
n

What is it?

Don't I Look Delicious?

HUMPHUMPHump

THICKSKINTHICKSKINTHICKSKINTHICK

googleyes nicebigmilky WARTYB○DYWARTYB○DY

sticky tongue poisonglands WARTYB○DYWARTYB○DYWARTY

B○DYWARTYB○DYWARTYB○DYWART

PALESLIMY BELLYBLOWNUP LIKEABALLOON

stringy   stringy

legs   legs

softwormtoes   softwormtoes   puddle
of piddle

What am I?

SNAKE
AND TOAD

Snakes use the meadow both for basking and hunting; their favorite foods are grasshoppers, earthworms, toads, and salamanders. When snakes outgrow their skin, they start the shedding process by rubbing their heads against a rough surface. Rubbing tears the old skin, which they wriggle out of like a sock. The result is fresh, colorful new skin. While they are shedding, snakes cannot see or hunt well and are very irritable.

Since toads are not strong jumpers, camouflage is their main line
of defense against predators such as snakes. Their thick, mottled, bumpy
skin blends in well with the leaves and grasses of the meadow. Other
defensive tricks include puffing up their bodies to appear larger, secreting
foul-tasting poison from the glands behind their eyes, and urinating
on their attacker!

Always Together

We tumble
         we twitter
we dip
      float
         and flitter
On thistle
     we rustle
        and whistle
          and bustle
Dip-dodging
       leap-frogging
we're birds
       of a feather
Like ripples
   like petals
      like clouds
         in wet weather,
like
   bright
       chips
         of sunlight
flung
   skyward
         forever
we're always
   we're always
      we're always
         together.

What are we?

An Apology to My Prey

I am deeply sorry for my huge orbs
of eyes, keen and hooded,
that pierce your lush
tapestry of meadow.

And my wings: I regret their slotted tips
that allow such explosive thrust;
their span that gathers wind
effortlessly, and of course their
deadly, folding dive.

Let me offer an apology, too,
for my talons, impossibly long
and curved, sliding so easily
through fur and feathers,
seeking, as they do,
that final grip.

And last, of course, the beak.
It does tend to glitter, I know—
a merciless hook,
a golden sickle poised over
your soft, helpless heart.

I'm so sorry. For you, that is.
All this works out quite well
for me.

What am I?

GOLDFINCH AND HAWK

Tiny yellow goldfinches are extremely social birds, flocking together not only during migration, but also all year long. Singing and calling cheerfully as they fly, groups of goldfinches feast on seeds of the meadow—thistle, sunflower, and dandelion—as well as bugs and caterpillars. In winter, male goldfinches lose their bright yellow feathers and turn a duller greenish brown to match their female mates.

The red-tailed hawk, on the other hand, is a loner. Except during mating and nesting season, it roosts, soars, and hunts in solitude. This large hawk is a supreme hunter, with powerful eyes that see color and movement from hundreds of feet above the meadow. When it spots small mammals, snakes, toads, birds, or even earthworms, it moves quickly to seize the prey with deadly talons. The red-tail will also steal prey from smaller hawks and falcons.

The Gray Ones

We are the tall ones with crowns of velvet
    the high-steppers
    the flag-wavers
We are the silent ones that browse at dusk
    the bud-nibblers
    the ear-flickers
The gray ones that linger at woods' edge
    Swift   Still
    Here   Gone
Eyes of glass
Hooves of stone

We are the ghosts
    of those
    who have come before
The gray ones
      Leaping
         Gone

What are we?

We Are Waiting
(a pantoum)

Our time will come again,
say the patient ones.
Now is meadow,
but not for long.

Say the patient ones:
sunlight dazzles,
but not for long.
Seedlings grow amongst the grass.

Sunlight dazzles
and the meadow voles dance,
but seedlings grow amongst the grass.
Forest will return.

Meadow voles dance
where once was fire,
but forest will return.
We wait patiently.

Once was fire.
Now is meadow.
We wait patiently.
Our time will come again.

What are we?

DEER AND TREES

Meadows are formed in many different ways. Sometimes a forest burns, is blown down, or is cleared for lumber, leaving open areas. Sometimes a pond or wetland dries out. Meadow plants move in and thrive in these open areas. Then come animals such as the white-tailed deer, which feast on new shoots, shrubs, and berries, but can fade back into the forest at any sign of danger.

The land is always changing, however. Tree seedlings take root in the meadow, and the slow march toward forest begins again. This constant change in habitat is called succession.

Glossary

abdomen In insects, the hindmost (and usually largest) part of the body.

camouflage Coloring or body parts that help animals and plants blend into the background and hide.

excrete To get rid of waste from the body.

exoskeleton A hard shell that covers some insects and other animals, protecting and supporting their bodies.

immune Being resistant to, or protected from, a toxin or disease.

migration The movement of a group of birds or animals, usually in spring or fall. In spring, animals migrate to a place that is safe for raising their young. In fall, they migrate back to an area that will provide food in winter months.

nutrient Parts of food that are important to growth and development in living things.

nymph A young insect, often looking like a smaller version of the adult but without wings.

pantoum A poem form ("We Are Waiting") in which the second and fourth lines of a stanza are repeated as the first and third lines of the next stanza. In the final stanza, the first and third lines of the poem appear in reverse order, so that the last line of the poem is the same as the first.

phloem Tubes inside a plant stem that carry food made by the leaves to all parts of the plant.

pollinator An insect that carries pollen from one flower to another, thus fertilizing the plants and allowing seeds to form.

predator An animal that hunts other animals for food.

prey An animal that is being hunted.

spume Another word for foam or froth.

succession The gradual, naturally occurring changes that take place in a community of plants and animals.

talons The long, sharp claws on the feet of raptors (hawks, eagles, owls), which are specially adapted for grabbing and killing prey.

ultraviolet A color just beyond violet on the color spectrum, with wavelengths of light that are too short to be seen by human eyes.

xylem Tubes inside a plant stem that carry water and minerals upward from the roots.